T0080375

FREAKISHLY CREEPY CREATURES

by Megan Cooley Peterson

CAPSTONE PRESS
a capstone imprint

Published by Spark, an imprint of Capstone
1710 Roe Crest Drive, North Mankato, Minnesota 56003
capstonepub.com

Library of Congress Cataloging-in-Publication Data is available on the Library of Congress website.
ISBN: 9781666355352 (hardcover)
ISBN: 9781666355369 (paperback)
ISBN: 9781666355376 (ebook PDF)

Summary: Outstanding photos combined with high-interest text describe a variety of creepy-looking animals, their diet, and behaviors.

Editorial Credits
Editor: Erika L. Shores; Designer: Hilary Wacholz; Media Researchers: Jo Miller and Pam Mitsakos; Production Specialist: Tori Abraham

Image Credits
Alamy: Nature Picture Library, 29; Getty Images: Jasius, 5, Jim Zuckerman, 11, Johner Images, 9, Thorsten Negro, 14; Shutterstock: Anna Veselova, 15, belizar, 4, Cassel, davemhuntphotography, 19, Jane Rix, 24, 25, Michal Sloviak, 6, NatalieJean, 27, Neil Bromhall, 20, 21, pr2is, Cover (bottom), reptiles4all, Cover (top), Ryan M. Bolton, 18, skifbook, 16, svetjekolem, 23, Vaclav Sebek, 7, Wirestock Creators, 13

Design Elements
Shutterstock: Cassel

All internet sites appearing in back matter were available and accurate when this book was sent to press.

TABLE OF CONTENTS

Creepy Critters 4

Creepy in the Sky 6

Creepy on the Ground 10

Creepy in the Water 22

Glossary 30

Read More 31

Internet Sites 31

Index 32

About the Author 32

Words in **bold** are in the glossary.

CREEPY CRITTERS

Bats that slurp blood. Spiders big enough to eat birds. Not all animals are cute and cuddly. Some are so scary you might scream! Get ready to meet some real creepy creatures.

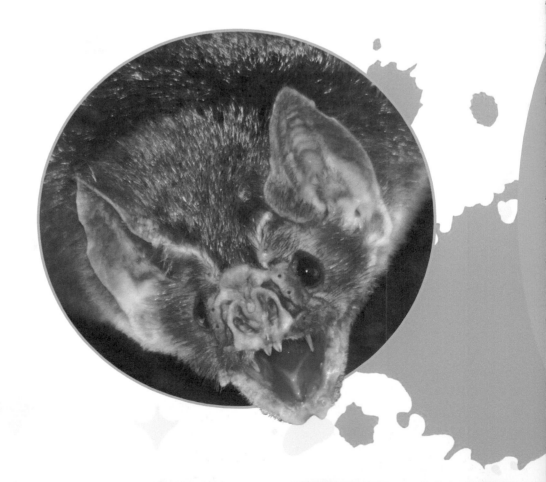

CREEPY IN THE SKY

MONSTER BIRD

The shoebill stork belongs in a scary movie. Its **bill** can grow longer than a football. These African birds use their bills to grab fish and turtles. Shoebill storks even pluck baby crocodiles right out of the water.

FACT
In the wild, shoebills can live more than 30 years.

HUNGRY FOR BLOOD

Vampire bats come out at night. These flying **mammals** are on the hunt. But not just any food will do. They need blood!

Vampire bats feed from sleeping cows, pigs, and sheep. They bite with teeth as sharp as razors. The bats lap up the blood for as long as 30 minutes. Then they fly away.

CREEPY ON THE GROUND

HIDING IN PLAIN SIGHT

A leaf with legs? Talk about creepy. Flaps of skin make the leaf-tailed gecko's body look like leaves. Many also have leaf-shaped tails. These geckos blend in with the forest floor. The geckos hunt at night. **Prey** can't spot them.

> **FACT**
> Leaf-tailed geckos live only on the island of Madagascar.

TERRIFYING TARANTULA

A big, hungry spider hides on the ground. A bird lands nearby. The goliath bird-eating spider waits for its dinner to come closer. Then this tarantula sinks huge fangs into the bird. The bird's insides turn to liquid. The spider drinks it up like a nasty milkshake.

FACT
The goliath bird-eater is the biggest spider on Earth. Its leg span is 12 inches (30 centimeters) wide.

WHAT BIG EYES YOU HAVE

The sun has set. And the spooky aye-aye has come out to feed. This **lemur** has big, bat-like ears. They listen for prey. Big, round eyes help it see in the dark.

Long, bony fingers grip branches. The aye-aye has an extra-long finger. It digs for bugs in trees.

TOO MANY LEGS?

A monster-like bug races along the forest floor. The giant centipede can grow up to 12 inches (30 cm) long. These bugs have 21 or 23 pairs of legs.

Giant centipedes are speedy hunters.

They catch lizards, mice, and bugs.

Two fangs deliver a deadly **venom**.

NIGHTMARE BUG

The tailless whip scorpion is the stuff of nightmares. It lives in caves. And it only comes out at night. A whip scorpion has 10 long legs and huge **pincers**. It grabs bugs and frogs with them.

NO CLOTHES NEEDED

Wrinkly skin. No fur. Huge teeth. Naked mole rats won't win any beauty contests. These African **rodents** live in groups underground. The queen mole rat rules the group. The other mole rats work for her. They raise young and keep the group safe.

CREEPY IN THE WATER

DON'T BITE!

What big teeth you have! Gharials have long, thin snouts. As many as 110 needle-sharp teeth line their jaws. Gharials snap their jaws shut to catch fish in rivers. Their teeth lock together to trap prey. Then they swallow their food whole.

> **FACT**
> Gharials have weak legs. They slide on their bellies when on land.

CREEPY CRABS

It's easy to see how the Japanese spider crab got its name. It looks like a huge spider creeping along the ocean floor. This crab is the largest on Earth. Its legs can reach 12 feet (3.7 meters) from tip to tip.

FACT
Japanese spider crabs can live more than 100 years.

BIG MOUTH

Open wide! The sarcastic fringehead has a scary smile. Its huge jaws hold sharp teeth and a purple tongue.

These fish live in seashells and even old bottles. They flash their gross grins to scare away attackers. Fringeheads also fight each other. They smash their mouths together. They do this until one of them swims away.

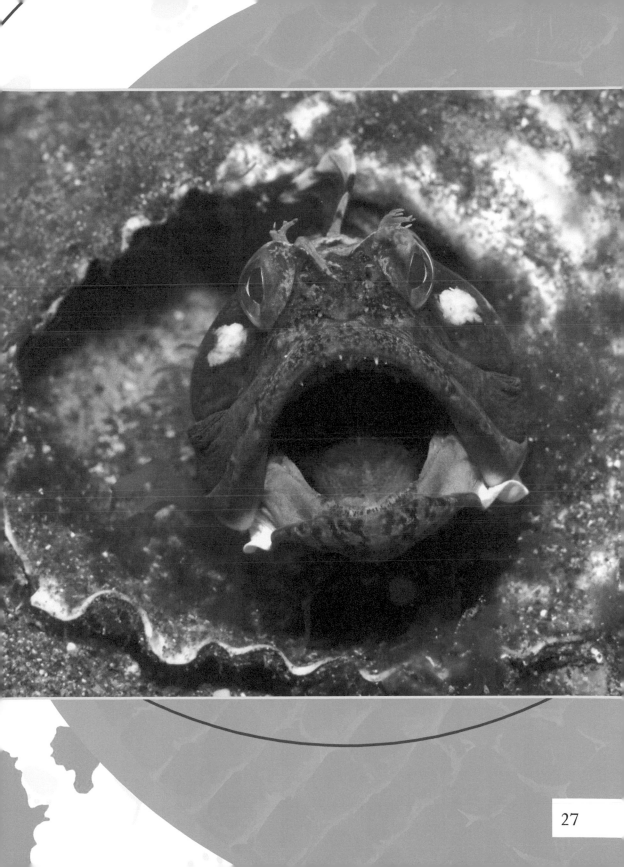

CREEPIEST FISH IN THE SEA?

Is that a fish or an alien? Black dragonfish swim deep in the sea. They have long, thin bodies. Females have teeth-like fangs. A feeler on their chin glows. They move it back and forth to catch food. Fish that swim too close get eaten up. Chomp!

FACT
Male dragonfish are much smaller than females. They have no teeth.

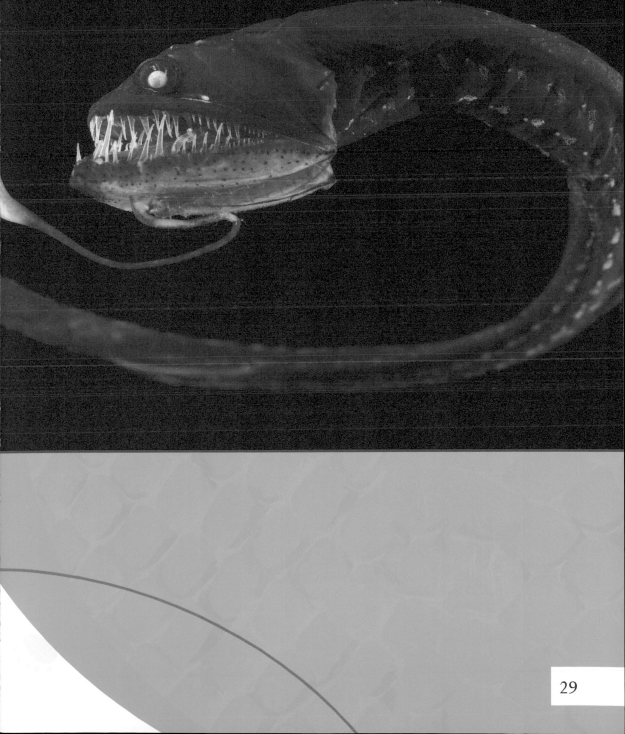

GLOSSARY

bill (BIL)—the hard front part of the mouth of birds and some dinosaurs; also called a beak

lemur (LEE-muhr)—an animal with large eyes and a long, furry tail; lemurs are related to monkeys

mammal (MAM-uhl)—a warm-blooded animal that breathes air; mammals have hair or fur; female mammals feed milk to their young

pincer (PIN-sur)—a claw used to grab and pinch prey

prey (PRAY)—an animal hunted by another animal for food

rodent (ROHD-uhnt)—a mammal with long front teeth used for gnawing

venom (VEN-uhm)—a poisonous liquid produced by some animals

READ MORE

Hyde, Natalie. *Animal Oddballs.* New York: Crabtree Publishing Company, 2020.

Knapp, Ron. *Bizarro Bloodsuckers*. New York: Enslow Publishing, 2019.

Sexton, Colleen. *Aye-Aye.* Minneapolis: Bearport Publishing Company, 2021.

INTERNET SITES

Cool, Not Creepy!
kids.sandiegozoowildlifealliance.org/stories/cool-not-creepy

Goliath Bird-Eating Spider
kids.sandiegozoowildlifealliance.org/animals/goliath-bird-eating-spider

Ooey Gooey Creepy Crawlies
kids.nationalgeographic.com/nature/article/ooey-gooey-creepy-crawlies-

INDEX

aye-ayes , 14

black dragonfish, 28

gharials, 22
giant centipedes, 16, 17
goliath bird-eating spiders, 4, 12

Japanese spider crabs, 24, 25

leaf-tailed geckos, 10

naked mole rats, 20

sarcastic fringeheads, 26
shoebill storks, 6, 7

tailless whip scorpions, 18

vampire bats, 4, 8

ABOUT THE AUTHOR

Megan Cooley Peterson has been an avid reader and writer since she was a little girl. She has written nonfiction children's books about topics ranging from urban legends to gross animal facts. She lives in Minnesota with her husband and daughter.